NEAR-GHAZALS

ACKNOWLEDGEMENTS

Thanks to the editors & publishers of the following periodicals & books in which some of these poems first appeared or will appear, sometimes in a different form:

The Long Island Quarterly, Seventh Quarry, Corona: A Pandemic Anthology (Edited by Gayl Teller), Forty by Two: Street Press Duets, which published the first forty of these poems in a chapbook along with Graham Everett's *Just This Very World (Street Press,* 2020), and to Joe Napora for publishing a limited edition keepsake of numbers 107-116 as *Near-Ghazals*. Thanks, too, to Karla Linn Merrifield for her reading of and help with the first 40 and for getting the word out on her blog.

Published in the United States
BullHead Books
509 North Main Street / Piqua Ohio 45356

ISBN: 979-8-218-18912-9

NEAR-GHAZALS

17 April 2023

For Anne Himmelfarb ~

Jack Means would like you to have this book. I would like you to like it, all 150 of these Near-Ghazals.

Enjoy, Dan

Dan Giancola

Dan G[illegible]

1

Because desperation is hard work
I try to do the inevitable well

I've got nowhere to go
& no one waiting when I get there

Algorithmically inundated
society's made a deep fake of our time

Shining like sclera in the dark
the bowl of a plastic spoon

from which I sip the moon

2

Every day's ephemeral
but moments don't fear letting go

Your loquaciousness depends
upon the boulder's silence

an exculpating breeze
tousling your coif

In a sheet of paper a thread curls
Renaissance fossil that tells me

I've opened again to the wrong page

3

Sunbathing beauties preen around the pool
thoughts cavorting in last night's bedrooms

Palm trees sieve breezes
I love women who go commando in cutoffs

People who tip   the wait-staff forgets
those that don't it scorns

You don't need a degree in Russian prison tats
to know Russians in Punta Cana

Wearing hip American tees they rarely *Hola!*

4

With new hearing aids rustling paper crackles like fire
refrigerator humming keeps entropy at bay

Two days after returning I shit the last
of my foodie vacation   grouper ceviche

Last year's hydrangea bloom looks like a sponge
tumbleweeds along the curb & takes flight

Green moss like jewelry box linings roll off the roof
spoors as old as the moon launch into the wind

I want to die as beautifully as autumn leaves

5

Today's class-actionable weather dithers
The dark has nothing to say to me

I'm as dry as the sky swept clean
by a breeze like Segovia's fingers playing oaks

A grey squirrel's cinnamon-dusted snout rhymes
with oak leaves yet fraying in January wind

In this age of untruth words matter more
than ever   I want an hour to dabble at your center

Look around   Do your due judiciables

6

Cold like a squatter enters skin & I run
a thousand thoughts down abandoned neurons

Sunset revision shimmers with editing marks
Clouds like smudged erasures await an archival wind

Like molten asterisks   welding sparks sizzle
a rattler rhumba that strikes eyes & disappears

Nothing any further in the past than the last moment
where   when we hungered for love

hate's absence brought no pleasure

7

Two mallard hens await drakes in a sump
where frogs choke on their own songs

Daffodils like paint spots warm & cheer the chill
sky like a sheet in need of bleach induces

Come evening I go home to nothing
no longer dream of your thighs' weathered leather

Moon like a garlic clove pinned to night's dinner jacket
I hear something open like a tulip in my chest

Yes   I am again ready for love

8

I want to be funny but you want money
salmon skin wallet bursting with mercury

Continuity grows threadbare   Was I ever
the child   the young man   I remember   Never

Stars like the rabble of a distant village hoist
acetylene flambeaux & march upon the inexplicable

Why is it we don’t teach peace
democracy now mere grist for the grift

Someday I’ll piss on Mitch McConnell’s grave

9

At night water like a poltergeist rattles my pipes
my pulse taking fright   a djinn speaking static

Silverfish in books gnaw holes like Neolithic runes
rhetoric that fails to pierce our ignorance

Among folding chairs applause scatters
Ask Lazzeri & Big O if time doesn't also greatness forget

Lost in an age of instant gratification
the time it takes to make things excellent

Drive toward a rising full moon to feel your own irrelevance

10

Weather's depressive epistles warn of pig
trouble in Little Latin & a slice for Mohammed

Be-hatted bearded be-bop pianist Monk steppin'
A lotta his compositions is classics now

You watch weeks pass like expiration dates
all night drinking the dreams of the doomed

Wear that water hat   man   where that water at
spell to spark dull embers in your charcoal soul

Where are you   whisky-chuggin' drunken dancin' gal

11

I awake in a strange room for the first time
watch sunlight like a friend walk across the floor

Abhor war because it renders peace moot
war & crows' contrapuntal aubades

The solemnity in which marriage begins
ends when the bride flings her bouquet

Change occurs moment to moment & within moments
atoms restless as motes afloat in sunbeams

Sometimes the neighborhood dies before you do

12

Rampant illness scours the populous & sours
air that seems to keen prefiguring tomorrow

Dawn sparks neighborhood camera lenses like pre
-dators' eyes tracking privacy's   like honesty's   extinction

While I'm downstairs practicing my ping-pong
prowess   porch-pirates pilfer my packages

Cold drizzle forces song from barometer bones
a slow blues that forecasts aching decades

I tear a thread from my boxers undergoing obsolescence

13

Mourning doves perch a limb like Incan gods
watch mockingbirds on an ashtray sip nicotine rain

In my sequestration afternoon bloats
like an unburied body & attention attenuates

The corpse's face chiseled by heroin grimaces
We can recycle neither breath nor time

Evening's exuberance will recede to quietude
Practice humility & own nothing if not dignity

All day sharpen heart's *duende*

14

I like to think neutrinos passing through our mass
take our mini-trinos with them to the edge of space

The door stays closed   ignorance its own quarantine
I talk to the past but it's not listening

A sky like Guinness foam portends good napping
but not a way to compost wasted hours

Social-distancing I'll become the last Japanese soldier
holed-up in an island cave forty years beyond war's end

I say I don't care but taut as piano wire anxiously thrum

15

Sun overhead bright as a celebratory sombrero
day has the look of the look in your eyes

Life lived remotely provides a virtual life facsimile
On this page I build a world more true than now

Light sutures past to future but between's all darkness
Rain has no expectations   Life yearns to live

Locked in our homes   Spring   we want your pheromones
your antibodies   your sun like a warm hand on our faces

Tonight I'll seduce myself with the last of the wine

16

In the moment sun's upper half dips below horizon's
seared meniscus   it inaugurates bird racket dispersal

A loner tooling around town in a loaner
punctures & punctuates a deeper social silence

Lives of poor decisions make decisiveness a liability
Best to hem & haw into futures booby-trapped with choices

Rain on a hermit's roof hones his misanthropy
In self's shelter war erupts against empathy

When I befriend distance the gouging begins

17

No society no shower I squat in my own stink
Solitude begins to pain like an in-grown nail

A self left with its quarrels declines from asceticism
walks in a drizzle under an umbrella of bird trill

I see a hyacinth-colored Nytrile glove
on the asphalt waving goodbye

Too much time alone bingeing serials & taking stock
of one's grudges only shrinks the soul

My Robinson Crusoe beard accentuates my new wattle

18

Outside my window daffodils nod with monotonous beauty
An Ur-squirrel scales an Eden oak jawing a copy of the first crocus bulb

In stems of wizened leaves a mystery worth study resides
but I turn inward like a penitent & subside

One can't have more fun right now than depilating
a hirsute razor or peeling kiwis with a butter knife

Like a parolee in an ankle bracelet I can't go far
inducing an ennui that renders vision an invalid

No one has touched me in over a month

19

Unlike a novitiate's willed cloister   an RNA strand's
tyranny imposes an ostracizing detachment

We are all once again third-graders eating lunch
alone & afraid in a new school's first day cafeteria

Wary as pickets cormorants black as distrust perch
marina pilings   wings folded like morticians' smocks

Waiting it seems as in prayer for the sun
my soul's an old dish-towel stained but clean

The mask I wear sieves life from treacherous air

20

An anchorite muses on his dysmorphic soul
here in this wilderness I call my home

Left with nothing but the vapid pap of my thoughts
I turn feral to feed upon moon's bloody tears

A woman with windowless eyes smalts
the sky with her laugh & asphyxiates the stars

Oracular erotic spring shakes my ipseity
another short chapter in the history of peace

Dan   you fool   there's always more wine

21

I am the nothing that loves the nothing you're not
the everywhere that takes me to a place not me

Wind rustling chimes in your eyes mutes me
Nothing I feel has not been felt before

Disaggregated citizens   we'll learn again to love
the world   the sun that slinks lynx-like through ivy

In shade that hums in cedars   I miss the handshake
& seats so close I sense my pulse in your throat

Stranger   stop   We want the same things

22

Libertarians   where's your vaunted Individual now
isolated & longing for herd immunity

Your gutted government is ill-equipped for crisis
power incredulous about its loss of power

Your Darwinian fatalism is inhumane
I'm with those who want to intervene

Alone on the water with a blanket of dark
I feel my every breath's immensity

In the light of numberless suns I wash my hands

23

An osprey nest atop a pine like a silvered
driftwood mast trails plastic like a kite-tail

Like a bunched napkin an osprey drops   hits Carmans River
& rises   sun-lacquered alewife entaloned in raptor mind

Ants again rove my kitchen countertops foraging
They scatter when with a finger I kill the first

Were it not for ego   my species' curse
I wouldn't mind dying like that alewife

those ants   one of the anonymous biomass

24

Egret stalks in a fallen oak's birdcage   stoops
eyes shadows in Forge River shallows

Tidal river runs out   creature on its belly
seems to slither   wind ruffling its nap

Skunk cabbage swathes the swamp green
shoots tight as straws unfurl broad leaves

Spring thunder surprises   future's oracular voice
Hail hits the deck like girls learning tap

The world's perfect save our perception perfection

25

Neighbors cut the maple that shaded my house down
a spring day welter of sawdust   pollen   decades of sun

Wood sawn & stacked   vacancies where the tree stood
filling with light as water seeks its own level in a void

Sun stored in my dermis flows in maple's phloem
a litter of florets like syllables of still-born leaves

As at ease in the tree as a trapeze artist   an arborist
subtracts limb by limb the tree from time

Twilight dyes blue the neighbors' white siding

26

Here in the present the past's version of the future
amuses us   all that space-age clap-trap

What's happened to the word *love* that people
now use it to refer to how they feel about a text

Punching monotony's clock the quotidian hunkers down
quiets the terror lurking just behind our acumen

Ignorance crusades to sniff out scapegoats
it can't see when blinded by what isn't there

Imagination's failures too often do us in

27

Goose on a reed mound broods her clutch   raising time
to time her head off her back   tenaciously patient

Fog like a dustiness spreads upriver with the tide
marsh descending in twilight to a chill

Sun through a skylight prints chair shadow on tile
For a moment my black dog again sleeps at my feet

I find a bird's nest built with twigs & plastic
thorns as menacing as shark fins guard its hollow

The nest fills with mind   the mind with emptiness

28

Here on this continuum eternity is our illusion
birth & death each nanosecond until space collapses

How many miles has the Great Blue Heron each day
walked as it stalks the riverbank for prey

Ants from nowhere each spring visit my kitchen like a time-share
& disappear   dead or moving-on   transcendental emigration

Box turtle on Wertheim trail sets its Porto-bunker
smackdab in the cindery middle to warm its plastron

shell markings pre-speech graffiti protesting a dream

29

Wherever this is it's what we do here
time the watch & pour the twine

When one stays home so much gets done
Waiting makes good weather for work

Garden worms await me & my shovel
scattered scraps to turn under & into

Donning a mask to market I'm as nervous as a cat
perplexed by a green avocado in my blue hand

Home   I awaken & lie back out of time

30

Gnat-cloud circles an invisible axis   describes
atomic energy in an amorphous   shaky hand

Mockingbirds roust from their cedar a crow
sounding its one note like a bad poet

Walking in thought not on the trail I'm walking
a black racer like a graphite pipe wakes from my reverie

& into budding underbrush snaps   turning perhaps
to validate my springing from its own sun-beclouded dream

& we part   blood into awareness stunned

31

I wake to my 70th day of solitary having kept myself up
all night   conversationalist I always dreamed I'd be

Virtual teaching only next semester spins my moral compass
Soul-crippled hypocrite   I'll join Mammon & take their money

Two ticks   dam & nymph   in my flesh begin to do their work
Nothing in nature thus far has hurt me more than people

The past is never around when you need it
memory useless coordinates to an ephemeral world

Without desire no future before us opens

32

I aimlessly drift through my house   a ghost
on the phone with someone loved long ago & lost

I have only myself to further examine
unplumbable me   myself as other   another mask

I begin to open cabinets & drawers best left shut
feel love-forsaken & forlorn   feed on self-pity to survive

I invite the moon in for dinner but it wastes not
its empathy on me   A green breeze through screens

ransacks the house out of which I've yet to sweep the spiders

33

Someone left beside the trail a turd for flies to dance upon
tissues fluttering   the white & brown flags of Assholia

Litter everywhere changing blue & white shrub-strung masks
gloves the color of every spring flower blooming in underbrush

A dogwood sheds petals   sun's parade ticker-tape
Oaks cast off catkins traffic sweeps curbside in umber waves

A snake like the shadow of a twisted branch with a ripple
as I near it disappears or a branch shadow twisted

like a snake with a breeze as I near it disappears

34

I breathe morning's silence   sip it like wine
quiet hinting at eternity between a mushroom's gills

The Great Egret like a slender milk-glass vase
strides low-tide Moriches Bay like a debutante

Wavelets collapse   hiss a whisper in the shingle
continuity's susurrus   sea ceaselessly reducing stone to sand

Overhead the day-moon like a nibbled cocktail onion
reflects a deafening silence as blue evening descends

I watch above my house a single cloud dissolve

35

Terns fishing fall out of tonight's sunset like kamikaze
or arrows shot from far-off unseen bows

hit the surface like hammers falling & rise
beaks clamped on killies shining like pieces of eight

It's so quiet I can see with my ear an insect
hum I took at first for my own tinnitus

Yes   peace does exist in the world despite George Floyd's
lynching & a Criminal-in-Chief tough-guying his way

out of the nation's highest office & into the hearts of haters

36

I *feel* getting older   want more quiet now not less
practice for the grave until only a grave's silence will suffice

I don't often recognize my own happiness but have no
trouble hearing halyards knock like cops on dreaming's door

In morning chill I awaken groggy with ill-remembered dreams
Later   I consider polka-dot roses abloom in the vase of the mind

Over ivy in solstice twilight's sinking gloam fireflies
blink like untethered buoys a-bob night's incoming tide

You search for a future on a fluid map destined for obscurity

37

Living fossils horseshoe crabs' carapaces host slipper snails & chitons
mate in Moriches Bay   image as eternal & elemental as the moon

About life's end I believe only there's nothing to believe
Life is the god whom we adore   to whom we make obsequies

Every new-born opens eyes into light already eight minutes old
will spend the rest of life trying to reclaim that time

Dancing around your backyard naked in hard dawn rain
you look up to find your lovely neighbor mooning you

The best nights are the nights we won't remember

38

A June sprinkle   a sunset & rainbow   clouds
like carp schooling across sky's looping tide

Honeysuckle like an agreeable corpse sweetens my beard
going out ushers in privet's mortuary astringency

Cremation or burial   Do I really need to choose or care
Let the living decide the dead-weight's fate

Like a storm long stalled offshore the quarantine finally lifts
People eat in restaurants again   neighbors host masquerades

A stowaway in this life   I'll have arrived when I'm found

39

I see with my ear the lies that sound in your eyes
Whenever you speak I watch truth die

Rain clatters on the deck like bones thrown to forecast
a future that sings of drought & deprivation

Summer cycles humid hours & sunshine with rain
& thunder   No need to worry the coiled hose

In Bellport Bay a key like a whale's green back breaches haze
vision breasting atmospheric waves to tag its flukes

Here at sea-level time's flood-tide pools at eternity's door

40

Weeks before the Fourth fireworks popping like bubble-wrap
might be gunfire because everything is like something else

Every embryonic second splinters infinitely
Probabilities abound in the future's following moment

I grow fearful getting older   Anything now can take me out
A plumeria drops a necrotic leaf soundlessly

Why strop our nation's divisiveness upon a virus
Feel free to do the esteemable   Wear a mask

You may live a while longer   Dan   so be careful with the whiskey

41

Down the page a poem's mute lines mime
You wish the poet paced his patter faster

Waitresses wearing masks convince that truth
& beauty reside in eyes   I open my heart's door

It's o'clock everywhere
& the future plots history's course

Wind whistles in the heart's empty chambers
A fine grit sands memory's proud edges

I live today to pay bills & take my pills

42

A mallard zig-zags like a drunk through creek's slush
-scrim   leaves bank to bank a last-to-freeze trail

The day's good deed   flinging a beached oyster into the bay
Sand fleas swarm a clam shell's pearlescent vacancy

An ice print   globular & indistinct   steps
like a dinosaur's fossil spoor into the future

I no longer care where goes the past & people known there
I have made my peace with transience

It's a good thing when one's shit floats

43

I open drapes to let my neighbors know I'm still alive
Through fog   a star like the dome-light in a sinking car

Under a streetlamp a guardrail like an alien alloy glows
Nothing but trouble when skies go goose-shit green

A neighbor leaves for   returns from work in darkness
tonight drags from the curb tympanic trash cans

Foam's amoebic shapes float thin as fish food
above its shadows straining like leashed dogs to lead

Felicity eludes me   *Donde es mi amor*

44

Poised today on oblivion's precipice   unmasked
party-goers double-down on disdain

A nation of fatalists courts extinction & ceding
free will gambles on an inside straight

I don't ask how much you drink because yesterday's
a long time ago & you can still whistle

November's rosy twilights fray my *joie de vivre*
It will be a long dark sad cold winter

You won't find this collection in stores

45

Hummocks at low-tide wear ice caps winking in the sun
Eggshells on snow   study on the hierarchy of white

A river breeze through lichen-spackled oak crowns flows
shaking rusty leaves that click like castanets

Here on shore the spoor of humans   swans & dogs
of heron   gulls & deer print a tale of termination

I'm heating heart's scriptorium with a cord of regrets
Your smile kindles the first flame

I imagined something different but like what I have made

46

The self-taught learning the moon often lose their way
but study the sun with a teacher & get left behind

At the intersection of speed & action
I hate having to suspend my disbelief

With primitive sophistication I admire nature's
elegant dilapidation   Rot does breed fecundity

Windblown cedars plait a braid above the bracken
What good will I be when I'm gone

You do it every day   Dan   but you're no good at dying

47

Some truths hide like scorpions in shoes
but you can't believe it because nothing anymore *is* true

The carton's date indicates on Valentine's Day
my milk will curdle as have all my loves

Forecasters predict snowfall from 2 to 16 inches
Might as well make that claim for every man

Sentimental as an archivist   I horde my life's detritus
I've lived   but nothing I've done has made a difference

Sideways blowing snow seats a snowman in a deck chair

48

I've done this year much gazing out windows
watching like a cat the world passing

Where will I find a lover of the unlovable
Ask any con-artist if *feeling* loved means you are

Romance begins with the loss & return of a dove-grey
glove   ends when children tire of their toys

Freedom of imagination may create artful conspiracies
but when truth from art departs ignorance ascends

Every time one writes a poem one writes about poetry

49

Oil truck drivers like divas don't like wet feet
Shoveling snow from the lawn I curse their daintiness

Prismatic icicles shine in sun & weep
brief winter flowers disappearing from the inside out

Morning rain polishes trail snow slick   I don't
hike so much as try   dancing toddler   to balance

I change my vaccination appointment four times
moving my way back from the future

Grey clouds above   black snow below   hangover in between

50

Doing nothing is what I stay busy doing
No work tougher than discerning one's thoughts

I am not insane   do the same things over
& over expecting the *same* results

Not *what* one does but how one feels doing it
Note the happy drunk   the suicidal philanthropist

Managing risk I tightrope the tension between
"You only live once!" and you only live once

Don't rush   Dan   Let the wine breathe

51

Contemplating the past we corrupt the present
proving mind can't be in two places at once

Are tears more evocative falling from blind eyes
I weep wondering which here we are

He knows the tools & paid his dues
With that body no one questions his lengthy beard

I'm tired of drinking alone   The bottle's
no talker   staring at me from a shelf

Seek the world's beauties not found in words

52

Night birds sing when stars lead their song
Urine stream shadow vibrates like a plucked string

That distrustful nagging cunt of conscience
says the things I value have no value

Madness generates no less truth than sanity
An imaginative lack creates a bureaucratic life

The cloud & its reflection in the lake—
Utterly different   exactly the same

I have done nothing & nothing has done me good

53

This verse traverses time
doing what it expects you to do

I ponder the photos
in which everyone is dead

Everybody—Everybody!—liked him
but nobody loved him

In a LaGuardia Airport terminal
a sparrow flits beam to beam

Unexpressed my love will spoil

54

We're getting used to more of less
adjusting to an age of attenuation

Palms rooted in time's mortal dance sway
On slippered feet waves *shush* ashore

Comfort   I hope never to find you   You open
banality's door   Time waiting with its child Entropy

Relativity   The Great Divider   blinds us to perpetual
ex vivo change   No thing stays the same

We're all learning to do less with more

55

Romance's apartheid now enforces solitude
My dry-docked heart lurches in its cradle

Dogs look smarter than some people   but no one
complains of pets taking people for granted

Older   I now suffer erasure's torture
marginalized but not yet gentrified

Beneath my skin I walk a ghost   conjure
ostracized spirits   join the overlooked & ignored

That hollow word   *love*   echoes in the wind

56

I have attained the age of atrophy
Everyday my flexibility & future disappear

My last relationship was like take-out sushi
too much wasabi & never enough ginger

Someone mows his lawn at 9 at night
Do not live among the simulacra

Wiping my ass I throw out my back
see in the mirror my hairline recede   my forehead loom

Mind moves perception as wind moves a shadow

57

A moose steps into the road from my mind's tree-line
Too late to brake I decide to pass through & do

Tombstones slam flat like dominoes   Epitaphs
slither like snakes off the stones then strike

Five a.m. cockcrow rends another dream asunder
I sink into that tortured aubade   lusting roasted fowl

We read old texts   Bible   Homer   Shakespeare
because therein lies evidence of our static nature

Nothing changes until humans do   Good luck

58

Moonlight waxes neighborhood car hoods
ephemeral adornment sunrise buffs to a shine

I drive a stretch of sun & shade   eyes dopplering
feel like I'm progressing into timelessness

Every day I make adjustments   fine recalibrations
compensate for my sense of accelerated disappearance

The moon's orphans hawk tears to rouge capitalists
who purchase that eternity with Bitcoin

Grill your plant-based burger   Dan   & decant the blue wine

59

Nature endows me with an Old-Man disguise
costume that frightens the child I still am inside

I am the words that leap off the page
What's not me   everything made to rot

Learning to see myself as others do
like learning a language without a grammar

In public I remain invisible   perfectly
fallible & gracefully inert   my body my tomb

At field's edge compost rows steam like oxen at rest

60

If I believed things were only different   none better
I could not believe Darwin   Don't give every kid a trophy

My son & I watch our team's NHL semifinal playoff
game 7   No matter the outcome   we'll cry

Aristotle knew a community's collective sadness
could lift a people from its hate & vengeance

Haughtiness is the chirping of the birds
confidence the owl's silence

It's so dope to write these selfies

61

Fifty years to the day my father died I again
watch lightning bugs' random balletic flickers

Under a gray humid twilight hydrangeas
bloom   empurpled as a squalling baby's face

Why this ancestry interest   What matters isn't
blood's origin but the country toward which it travels

Triple digit real-feel melts intention   saps
the laugh-track's humor   sets a carcinogenic haze

Overhead evening purls   river of cool fire

62

Surfers' heads bob like seals in the sea
but beach heat shrinks vision where sand becomes air

A photo's faces commemorate antique gestalts
The print obeying gravity slumps in its frame

The universe filled with suns & so dark
yet here a miracle   light in a housefly's eye

A flag's reflection waving in a window   frail
iteration   simulacrum distilled to transparency

Want has disabled many a conscience

63

At the launch boats idle   No one wants
to awaken the swan at the top of the ramp

All day thunderstorms threaten but never arrive
unlike the anger erupting to ruin our walk

Crabbers line a dock   dip nets   bait string with chicken livers
On the rails hunch crows & gulls awaiting opportunities

A near-by bird's coloratura helps cheer
my contemplation of our hypoxic Great South Bay

Love   despite your mission creep   Dan will reenlist

64

The porch-light brings nothing but bugs
does nothing to mitigate my clumsiness

A talking head claims kelp's the new kale
I'm paying these fuckers to pitch me!

This privet flower   one of billions now in bloom
one like any other   makes itself known to my nose

I watch the distance from which darkness descends
Free from freedom I revel in my own insignificance

Follow the energy   You'll lay low in the grave

65

Light in the guitarist's glasses wobbles
as in a projector lens   the new cinema

A green mirage swallows the pink asphalt
I'm nostalgic for a future I will not see

My signature tells you nothing   one letter
followed by a squiggly line under a dot

Back from extinction bison now browse former ocean
floor to furnish your table with meat   Stick a fork in it

Driving west I get younger chasing the sun

66

Crossing the country like a nomad in my car   I say
my rest-stop prayers   listen to idling semis seethe

Homeless meth-heads beg under Help Wanted signs
I point this out to one & he flips me the bird

Solitude's student   I learn to sound the depth
of silence's heart   that resonant slum

Midwest airwaves praise God & ask for his love
but God answers only with static

Alcohol   religion   humans escaping their deathfear

67

Young girls smoking at the rest area have no clue truck
drivers watching their long tan legs burst into flame

No more night travel   Even with readers
map roads at my finger's tip dead-end in oblivion

Gettysburg, PA, July 3rd, 1863
Imagine the vultures

Enter home upon returning from a trip & find every
-thing changed although nothing has been moved but you

No one survives an insistence upon personal freedom

68

If you live long enough you will lose
everything   Get used to it

Release attachments as you would a rope
Simply open your hand & let rope slip your grip

Life   ephemeral as a meal   insists you savor its flavors
Don't live like coins on a dead man's eyes

No meaning to life other than what we create
An archive empty of scholars has no utility

Savignon blanc   how do I stop being myself

69

I watch stars fall across your pupils
know I must learn to love what I hate

Blue-jays tussle over eggshells   spearing halves & flying off
One lights out like a motorcycle cop   white helmet shining

So long since I've lain with a woman
Her small tight ass like a ballerina's   I want it

From a Moriches Bay bulkhead I watch stingrays pass
like flying sand as you watch them pass across this page

Another tortured dream of trouble troubling my dreams

70

A brown leaf skitters over pavement   creates
sound not unlike the scratching of a record's final groove

I killed a tomato plant & a marriage with neglect
but I won't apologize for my mosquito pogrom

I catch the sun on my tongue   spit fire
where I walk   I cool down later chugging the dark

Along with fast-food bags   bottles & cans
Mastic romantics litter streets with dreams

A feral cat fearing domesticity limps into the woods

71

If success remains hard to sustain   why aim to achieve it
We hear it weeping at its apex   tragic hero about to fall

Some women in dreams of art try to break & bridle
wild men like horses they will ride with iron hands

To those who say mask & vaccine mandates abridge freedom
I say protest instead *no shirt   no shoes   no service*

A lifelong resistance to bureaucracy results
in scads of paper piled high *on* the filing cabinet

A paddleboarder might be Buddha serenely oaring

72

Certainties accumulate then atrophy   Lucky
we are to meet the dark with a truth or two

Each moment a moment passes a moment begins
Time earth's tilt & turn as we orbit eternity

Nothing worse   neither death nor taxes   than expectations
Assemble your cast-offs to build a room in hell

Your mojo seeks for its expression a funky dojo
place where the way originates in terminus

Ah   Dan   you fool   go fuck yourself

73

Nature fires us first   After   no clay's malleable
Culture's relief etchings reveal Nature's designs

Young molted horseshoe crab shells like sad   mis
-matched children's thrift-store shoes litter the tideline

Mullet mill against a bulkhead   diaspora
run out of future   Bluefish return to pursue the moon

Changing sex   not nature but art   In mind you've always
been what you now are   at heart you'll always be what you were

Nothing in nature changes its nature   Should we

74

Walking the Nissequogue's low-tide banks at dawn
Do fiddler crabs salute me or the sun

A killie school like notes in a symphony's score
turns at our approach   fluid melody

September   & wind speaks differently in oaks
rustling now like taffeta   paper bags   & tulle

One comes to a place in life where one needs help
but rarely arrives at the place to ask for it

Wine ages as well as yourself   Dan   but less bitterly

75 *for* James "Jimbo" Carvella (1949-2021)

Bunker churn dark spots siphoning comb jellies
the breathing sea's blind transparent eyes

As I read a book of Gary Snyder's   a moth
folded like a tiny fan falls into a poem

An inexplicable law of attraction dictates
a kook will always find another kook

Short Beach beach plums as numberless
in my mind as sand ripen like Liz Taylor's eyes

Tomorrow   Danny   you might just wake up dead

76

Fall flirts first with feeling   in the marsh
flicks cordgrass spikes with flame

I clear an overgrown corner   hack & slash
impose humanity   brutal translation   on wild roses

When did love become a foreign language
I no longer speak or understand

Fog fondles my flesh   frets my mystery
of bones   a mind apart from mine

The future warms & I feel its frostiness

77

Sometimes   despite tasking ourselves to get things done
moongazing through opera glasses is all we achieve

Above newly-mown soccer fields
dragonflies hunting poetry hover

A sole scuffed & soiled on pavement asks
if we can comprehend a shoe's exhaustion

Natalie Portman's Dior commercials assure me
I'm not only breathing but still in beauty's thrall

Some folks don't never get the love cure

78

We cheerfully inoculate our pets against disease
no longer love ourselves enough to do the same

A writer's journal with doodled over
hatched out blotted lines   consciousness scars

I watch Jupiter weep moons   wonder
if Love is not afoot dancing a reel

Blue-jays spearing grubs in my gutter fling
leaf debris   clear a way for the hunt & the rain

Natalie Portman   Ha Ha   Keep dreaming   Dan

79

I ask the wind one night where it is bound
I circle the world like a dog looking to lie down

The cracked red plastic dustpan & bent-bristle
broom   two faithful servants I have to let go

Preventing controversial speakers from appearing
on campus proves the left as fascistic as the right

Fire Island diet   a skinny martini   three Zippys
a glass of Malbec   a Lone Star   & a Sea Breeze

As usual   Dan   you're half right & all the way wrong

80

While my thoughts migrate intellectual savannahs
the moon limps like a crudely hewn clog across the sky

In Vermont's North Kingdom we watch leaves die
ephemerality visually textured

In a photo the sight of my bald head shocks me
like poetry   perceiving the everyday anew

Maine locals gather for burgers & cribbage
tweak tourists with GLUTEN-FREE FIREWOOD

Truth's more important than your right to lie

81   *for* Henry Honigman (1934-2021)

Your stardust imploded   your spark
lost in life's tidal surge & suck

You taught me to fish   chop wood   mix cement
instilled in me a work ethic I can't shake

In your eighties you'd leap from your anchored boat
swim the river to shore   fully alive

Even your laugh had an accent   came from your belly
That's when your face opened like a child's

You're water's sound now   ever breaking on the beach

82

A swan armada cruises in a phalanx up
the Terrell River   gang of toughs patrolling its turf

Hudson River pilings black & broken as a bum's
teeth as beautiful today as a model's smile

Although I'm fading like a rainbow
I celebrate the mystery of all we do not know

Dead leaves we are that fall into a brook
& swirlingly get swept away to sea

Fix what you can   Dan   & replace the rest

83

American Avocets run the shore to siphon seeds from foam
taste traces yet of Homer's stardust in the sea

Long Beach twilight   a cargo ship necklace on the horizon
glitters   flights to Kennedy wobble into view like stars

Torn between duty to the living & the dead
I miss your wake   Life takes me elsewhere instead

All night surf's concussive boom echoes   sluices
shreds   the waves' workshop making new beach

When the nor'easter arrives   Dan   open a Malbec

84

Like dreams the future arrives unbidden
Survival means surrendering control to change

In thought time slows   in action speeds
Attention equals elasticity

Off a deep-woods path I encounter a doe
watch a universe drain in her eyes black holes

Without temporal context infinity   that far
-off place   is myth   It's here in the song sparrow's skull

Dan   what you need now's a jolt of dopamine

85

I can't comprehend how leaves falling through woods
can sound louder than a bounding buck

That Romantic dream   *Objectivity*   cannot exist
because reality throbs with flux   defying measure

Older now   I feel pushed to the margin
forced to inhabit society's negative space

Moriches Inlet in November drifting spot for bass
I catch this line   *keepsake from the concrete-colored sea*

You'll never master   Dan   imagination's vastness

86

Fall's bright dying each leaf
effusive encomium attesting to the way

My only child almost died   woke from a coma
to ask for his shoes   He wanted out

Cultivate restraint   that human trait   with practice
produce patience   forgiveness   peace

Fall inlet waves cymbaling   wind
& tide foes   Nothing out here thinks about God

Raise your glass   Dan   & toast chaos

87

Nothing seems heavier than the silence
of a married couple's solitudes

So many people oppressed by the past's
accumulated static nurture their hurt

If *now* is always   time is stasis
its movement bureaucracy's first invention

Is my insignificance true or a delusion
maintained by a lonely wounded ego

It takes a lifetime to learn how to live

88

An oak's crown casts a dark net   sifts
winking stars from currents of earthdrift

Maples kindle flames that crackle in the distance
Oaks burgandize   I pale   appleflesh

In flight two swans morph into Concordes
but landing on the river resume life as swans

You will never be satisfied lunching with beautiful
women   watching their voices swimming like fish

Taste the dream in every dram of whiskey   Dan

89

Staring at copper trees I wonder if the world
now has fewer leaves than pennies

Thirty degrees this morning   A mosquito
bangs a window on wings of frost

Looking at my books   all that energy & learning
each a link in a chain that enslaves me

Not stories but gleanings from the stopflow
mind a dizzy stall   moving & still

Your true wealth   Dan   laughter & simplicity

90

Looking for clues to the afterlife   I fall into myself
find there a brown leaf floating on a vernal pond

Rain ends & dawn turns drops depending from ivy
into prisms   existence a trick of the light

I watch the season's first snowflakes   distance
between them shifting like intimacies

Waking early I watch day come on   no sound
but my tinnitus   peace & chaos of a tolling universe

You feel most free   Dan   when you don't believe anything

91

No one knows how I see what I see
not even me   & there's the trouble with reality

The journal in which I write   no heavier
with inked thoughts than when empty

I'm just trying to make it to the next day
I don't always have to be doing

November's icy gray spit   the wet cold
When have we ever been warm in the sun

Thinking about time   Dan   you lose it

92

His righteousness stands in him like an iron bar
Nothing said will ever open his mind

I wake from a dream of grief   begin writing
jokes   laughter turning soon to tears

Good morning   Horniness   milady   I await
my glimpse into your abyss   my retreat   the repeat

I begin to tabulate life's regrets
regret only having failed to trust myself

Wherever the past goes   Dan   leave it there

93

Critics agree   her body language creates literature
She moves like a line of type across a page

Tradition   father of banality   never suffers
change   pooh-poohs the new   eats apostates

Low tide empties all but a thread of the Terrell River
An explorer walking mudflats reads the river's bio

Like a Neanderthal I spend the night with one light
cold fire by which I sound imagination's depths

A muse sleeps in the wine awaiting your taste

94

Cold morning light quakes   wind composing
melodies with shifting notes of cloud

In the blockchain multiverse who will tokenize
my poem   father that provenance of light

One train of thought derails   another leads
down this cul-de-sac   because we die we love

Christmas Eve eve & through the cold falls snow
perfunctory & sparse   brief as joy

Each of us wears a visitor's pass in this world

95

Ours is a life of blurred lines
shaky emanations of sequestered energies

They can't hear me   I know but I still
talk to my dead friends   ask How's the party

Yeah   that's what I said   but no one owns
a chord   & Ringo stole his splashing cymbals from the rain

And distrust the wisdom of people who dance
when we cry   laugh when they lie   smirk when we die

You must learn   Dan   to smile more & reformat awe

96

Resolutions come & go but problems remain
addictions proving the most loyal friends

Chimney smoke rises into impoverished sky
spirals   stalls   pools   & then   snow

Who claims a writer cipher   *sans* agency
is a mystic & a liar   Art is not found but made

Your emotions flood their banks like a blocked
laconic rill   slow & reflective   not deep

Purging language creates a cleft tongue

97

Tomorrow's already yesterday   A moment ago
recedes into the centuries   Now looms

Whitman loafs in the soul's circuitry
harvesting cans & sparking scrub fires

Freezing rain ticks like a cooling oven   drains
gargle the trickle   We've all gone viral

Lately   an old bald white man is no one to be
but I'm happy to wake some mornings with a hard-on

Remember   Dan   the best things have no mass

98

Don't respect the perfunctory
love-child of boredom & disregard

Words evolve new meanings but don't shed the old
Listen with reverence for what yet resonates

With a remote in hand you wake in last
month's replay paralyzed by expectations

Rain skips like dice across car hoods
reminding me I failed at love

Things come together   things come undone

99

Leaves layered metamorphically in ice
will as slides of rot metaphorically suffice

I've outlived two fathers   told one dying
that I loved him uncertain he could hear

Don't jinx my jinx   leave me my grudge
Wrongs live long in the mind of a judge

Freedom's a bank account from which most
withdraw few funds   accumulate no interest

Our rights   a problem when they get in power's way

100

Topicality's provocations sunset with sunset but I
in evening's bright silences soak enjoying non-time

A flock of birds lifts from bare trees to fly
like pepper spilled across a tablecloth of fog

Impending snow's dense hush muffles
death's menace & the juju it adds to our mojo

Vaxed boosted & Covid-fatigued I head out
thinking today I'll drop my mask & let love find me

You get closer to self Dan as it gets further away

101

Not the frame upon the wall
but perception that is crooked

Winter sun on chill emptiness
the cold at the heart of loneliness

Lost arts   dressing well & discretion
Honesty's slovenly   negligence messy

Riding on a palindromic highway high
you inchoately enter the never-not-was

I try to write but nothing tastes right

102

Does wind shape the cliff-side pine
or pine have its way in the wind

Yes   you tend houseplants but can't say
they thrive   can't say how they survive

With any luck our children will foil
our best intentions & become themselves

Spring & a few things demand repair
I shrug & slog through till fall

God   clay   breath   how did it all go so wrong

103

From where I sit today Mariupol
looks like a city on the moon

Roots thick as serpents snake
across a trail   derail those looking up not down

When a screw in a pair of reading glasses
loosens it will rarely seat tightly again

All my life I've been eating poetry
& look how thin I am

Resigned to happenstance the mind dances

104

A first few drinks to let the devil dance
Orthodoxies atrophy until the blues is all we got

Easier to leave someone behind
when you yourself have been abandoned

I'm still feeding time to my blood's antic banshee
because thought often can't get where it's going

Not supply chain issues   A bar charges
a buck to drink my whiskey neat

The arts offer a haven for the neuro-diverse

105

Dollar's getting thin in the economic gym
Business fingers the buck's sweatpants' pockets

If you feel compelled at some point in life
to ask for respect   you haven't earned it

May it be said that a swan flying across
a road casts a shadow that is also flying

Crypto mines greedily suck the grid's nipple
Your groove's octane powers Camaros

Don't forget   Dan   the dead are not hard to find

106

As cold and formidable as God   Moriches Bay in April
lies at my feet like a sheet of tarnished armor

I wish for diaphaneity   to become pervious
oracle through which passes light & truth

Next week I'll know what
I should have said last week

What good does it do to secure
a financial future at the present's expense

I found peace when I stopped pimping my poems

107

I watch my Wall Street pension hemorrhage
A future of comfort & ease disappears

33 billion to Ukraine while the homeless
here die with democracy on the street

My check for a glass of bourbon includes
a two-dollar charge (plus tax!) for an ice-cube

Christ & corporations infiltrate our government
Difficult now to believe in even the pretense of liberty

Hey Dan Don't take any wooden ideals

108

When it's March in May as it is today
time stutters & blooms stall   rebirth in reverse

A week following the Supreme Court *Roe* leak
infant formula cannot be bought in stores

Wind makes trees flail as if with Pentecostal spirit
but the breeze can't blow the light from the leaves

Trouble is   a precedent corrected must assure
more liberty   not a return to repressive superstition

Open another bottle   Wine rarely looks back

109

I will one day like a log rot out of time
but today write not to see but *feel* eternity

How quickly recedes the recent past   Two
years ago feels as far away as Christ

Seconds like commas chop & separate
us from coherence   from ever-present *is*

A businessman must have invented counting
In a dream I smile sawing off his fingers

Only species that believe in time destroy themselves

110

White dogwood petals daub the lawn
like brushstrokes   spring's ticker-tape parade

All night on the lawn dogwood petals
shine   shards of a shattered moon

Breezes shear petals from the dogwood
drift a dune across my windshield

The dogwood petals form a puzzle I
can't fathom & will never reassemble

Dogwood petals   dream scrip stardust   throb

111

Take a quantum leap into dream yoga
Let sleep straighten your spine

All our lives we roll the dice   note
with hindsight the past is short on hope

Irises chug sun down their bearded maws
Lacking dignity they keel over   drunk on heat

Congress cares more for guns than children
May the deads' howling bedevil the kleptocrats' sleep

Time again for art to flex its muscles

112

Dusty June morning light   A numinous lemon
down traces trees' edges on the air

Blossom-blow in my hair reminds me of snow
dreams where the cold preserves dead faces

I used to find you by going inward
but now my heart is a cold   empty cave

The muse is a stuck-up   gold-digging bitch thinks
the poet   sipping a thirty-dollar margarita

All the past does   Dan   is recede   Let it

113

Crossing the Chesapeake   dragonflies hitch rides
on our jib sheet   & again I'm a delighted child

Is it enough to wonder about the wonder
of stingrays airing their black fin-tips   It is

Through a map of the heavens printed on river
glass   a fish leaps to feed on the stars

Dolphins like grey commas punctuate
the waves but who knows what waves say

People need tell-tails to show when they're full of wind

114

How like the universe my night lawn looks   grass space
-black   clover blossoms bright as suns   fireflies falling stars

Summer rain falls in straight grey lines like hanging fabric
For a few hours we exist in damp gauze

A storm's ovation hurls red & green seaweed   eel grass
on sand   creating the sea's expressionist painting

Oyster & cherrystone   quahogs & mussel shells litter
the beach   but only razor clam shells smirk

No poem when *vin ordinaire* fails to delight

115

Summer's swampy humid doldrums enervate
Heat swells cells & nakedness can't cool

A flicker grubs a mulberry's dead limb
scoots around as if on wheels twisting invisibility

When you think about the future don't squint
A few years   fine   but no one needs forever

Practicing poetry's craft I disappear
reemerge without a voice & empty pockets

One new rule   no frowning in the pool

116

By firefly light I read the moon's gauzy script
hear with a bat's eyes rain's first *splop*

White wine & lunch all week with women
I take no other meal   feel my powers galvanize

A least bittern stalks in its yellow
wellies a canted jetty stone to fish the flow

I too dream of a striped-bass honey-hole   sad
miracles   & mermaids with amorous genitalia

Tonight   Dan   you rest in the ineffable   Take note

117

Today's sky like grandma's too-often-washed
gingham dress enfolds us in its terrible benignity

What happened to my son's half skull-cap
Did he dream in his coma of it turning to ash

That Uvaldi cop who thought to sanitize
his hands will never disinfect his conscience

No one asked but I say make the Seditionist-in
-Chief eat his hair   on TV   then hang him

Yes   wine will soothe the world's vulgar indignities

118

Long after the faucet stops gushing   the sink drain
speaks to me   my friend's voice hanging from his rope

Difficulty is difficult to state simply
Simplicity is too difficult to state at all

I almost walk into a sprinkler soaking the street
What perfunctory stay stops me from cooling off in this heat

The past is always also *now*
It's always/never tomorrow again

We spend life tuning-up   When does the music begin

119

Birds eating cherries shake leaves hopping branch
to branch   choreograph a lightshow shadow dance

Zooming past me an older woman driving
applies eyeliner   Does vanity ever age out

I thumb an ant into *not*   Forgive me   Nature
Explain why I can't seem to live with you

We watch again Freedom kill   Is it best
to be a coddled pet or a short-lived wild beast

Hope is for losers   Dan   Struggle

120

Sunday morning Cessnas buzz & drone above my roof
insects waking me from my silent dream solace

This morning I reread what I wrote last night
to learn if it's as good as I recall   Nope

Everything changes but the fact that everything
changes   even your despair if you would let it

Don't gaze in the mirror wearing reading glasses
They magnify your slumping face's every line & wrinkle

Dan   open that old wine before it turns

121

Soul won't return   It's only self's sense
of self & it dies when you die

Ants on August first in my clean stainless
steel sink teem searching for a queen

We get our rights not from God   who
does not exist   but from our faith in fair play

Nature's hierarchy holds its balance between
prey & predator   the life of death that fuels all life

Despite the world's complexity   it's a simple place

122

Each night   orb-weaver   you're at my door but where
do you go daytimes   the hydrangea or the gutter

When the lawn service mows down my peppers
how can I not begin again to cut my own lawn

To be always among people results in terrible artists
but also the empathetic & most popular   Which are you

After downpour air more humid than before
I stroll through melted glaciers that crowd my lungs

Not much of a life x-ing out dates on your calendar

123

Two marsh hawks skim pine-tops & gyre
hunting chipmunks that scurry in & out of time

Short Beach sunset low-tide & the home-made boat
floating Henry's ashes explodes into remembrance

I wake from a nap believing I'm at a train
crossing when in fact a halyard rings a mast

Her nipples stiffen into thimbles   Where
do we go when pleasure enters the body

Hey   Graham   No one cares if I'm speaking to you or me

124

My philosopher muse rubs my endorphins right
I feel the meaning of Being course through me

Why make distinctions   light *is* leaf
Intuitive winds rustle leaflight

We phase into mega-drought   Winds dessicate
Our futures burn   We pray the waters will rise

When will this poem let us in   It doesn't
belong here & does   ramifies as you read

Not wine's job to tell the truth   Invent it yourself

125

A teen on the train pokes her phone   jounces
a scabbed knee   She has yet to shave her thighs

Hard as fists & grass green   August tomatoes
refuse to ripen   It took me years to grow up

A pregnant woman strolls the beach   toddler in tow
She whispers when he dawdles   *getting' time to go*

September soon   We'll wait a week to jam
beach plums   their sun-plumped sweetness in abeyance

Ah, to live always on the precipice   poised to fall

126

A swallowtail from nowhere swoops past me   dis
-appears   makes me feel I've drawn the spade ace

Neighbors' barbeque smoke speeds through my screens
beeves stampeding   pigs flying   chickens crossing the road

Still here   orb-weaver   off-web-center in battered
silk tatters   hunger's martyr with off-spring distended

When I pick the tomato I craved it proves blighted
Cankered splits & black rot spots teem with ants

A sunflower sags like the head of an old man napping

127

I wake to clatter like tacks scattered   a few
seconds of drought-rain slaking my dream-thirst

Time I keep in my pocket & spend freely
a cash wad   my inexhaustible stash of *now*

Along the boulder-strewn shoulders of the Sound
a wasp hunts crickets over pulverized eons of sand

We stumble into a future we presume exists
When tomorrow arrives it will be today   always today

We make suffering   Everything else comes from the stars

128

A sunflower's bract droops over my fence
Seeds fall like teeth from its face

Cloaked in Democracy   business denigrates
reason to continue duping the stupid

An ambulance arrives next door
The driver loads Death in the rear & departs

Russian oligarchs starve humanity
squeeze from Putin's folly the final ruble

We tend toward entropy   Bear up

129

At the dock fry as translucent as truth school   synced
to turn together until a snapper leaps & they scatter

Once indicative of sailor   outlaw   convict   whore
tattoos today denote the bourgeoisie & soccer moms

A jellyfish with mushroom-like bell trails a trinity
of tentacles   No   wait   that's a paper-towel afloat

Suburban crime doing all that need be done   wasting
water   befouling bays   poisoning soil   to keep lawns green

In the wine tonight I taste guano & the grub

130

No system less patriotic than capitalism
It would sell Lincoln's soul to make a buck

Fuck those loser market lemmings dumping stock
in response to moves made to improve America's economy

I once had money but it works like dope
I must break my habit   narrow my scope

Moonlight equitably spreads its currency   scrip
with which we fund portfolios of desire

Bitter cheap wine tastes fine at this time

131

Cloud skyline   yellow & blue   vaporous city
on a hairline poising   vacant & opaque

Late summer day drowses along Forge River
Reeds bow their heads to kiss the cooling earth

On the workbench of the beach surf exhausts
itself   incessant thuds heard on a factory floor

Rain like spilled gravel quiets crickets   who soon
after in moon's anywhen afterglow again make song

Dawn's benevolence can numb you   Wake up

132

Because tea leaves tonight lie mute in my mug
I read instead what steam foretells of dissipation

Women in Iran burn *hajibs* protesting theocracy
Elsewhere a spacecraft nudges an asteroid's orbit

On Bellport Bay's turbulent table wind shakes
out whitecaps like napkins   I reach for my knife

A brushstroke of old ivory on velveteen canvas
the parenthetic moon awaits your kiss

Evenings you doomscroll a hole in your empathy

133

Like something from a tin can snipped   a spider
-cricket perched on a plate's rim sips a tomato seed

I'm still walking around & it's already today
Tomorrow   a ways off   distills nightmares from the fog

Any wayfarer knows hindsight does nothing but blame
On foresight we move forward   annealed by scars

October residual hurricane rain   low pressure
I'm in no mood for fools   feel as empty as a Hopper

Only after whiskey   Dan   do you accept infinity

134

Across from me out a train window a woman stares
Neon graffities her face   Litter flies in her eyes

A metal detectorist listens to the beach he sweeps
for coin sonatas   ring roundelays   gold oratorios

Dogs & children love you   Adult women   not so much
Spirit rides a body hard   Sorrow makes no excuses

Although I now enter my canescent senectitude
You may not tell my blood   still warm   what to do

On cankered days wine dies on your tongue

135

Across the ceiling darts a spooked bird's shadow
No   Only a pull knob my hat knocks into flight

Light out   light on   no difference to crickets
whose ratcheting cheers your return from the world

You watch a movie that makes you want to make
a movie you would watch & want to make

Transfixed by death's beauty   the matriarchs
watch leaves transform from life to life

You   too   Dan   Don't forget   You   too

136

What waste   acorns by traffic crushed & ground
into flour that will never feed the world

Because your body doesn't know you well
it must be made to understand denial

Some stumblebum tans in train station sun
No ride arrives   but he's already gone

Oil dear   thermostat buried   you inure your
-self against cold walking half-naked through snow

A kiss   Dan   could open a door out of time

137

A jay can't perch a narrow feeder's edge & so
beak in seed hovers like a hummingbird in slo-mo

Above me on the tunnel's tile ceiling a steady
winking tail-light slipstream stalls into traffic

Ducks appear fast flapping   create polite applause
then disappear into blinding Moriches Bay fog

An oak leaf like a wizened palm cups rain
I sound its shallow clarity & sip the cosmos

In a neighbors' pool cover puddle the Milky Way seethes

138

Red & yellow leaves impaled on green under
-growth glow like June blooms & it's spring again

Call no knife yours until   flashing like a shy
smile   it tastes your blood   Then tell it goodbye

On an October refuge trail two Spanish women sing
keep time scuffling like maracas fallen time

Robins gorge autumn olive berries   leap withe
to withe   drop & twist like acrobats sugared up on joy

That wine won't open itself   Dan   Get busy

139

The life we shared sinks into the past as into a sea
the sun   most dismorphic just before it disappears

Yes   people must choose happiness because un
-happiness is humanity's default emotion

Who feels the vibrato aurora shimmer in numena
inherent knows death like time is but a construct

A shadow wafts & whirleygigs   I think monarch
but see only an oak leaf beginning its own migration

Stop drinking whiskey when the shots cease to burn

140

Some mornings I taste the sun   hold it
on my tongue until it ripens into wine

A post-coital retirement hotwires his Powerball
dream of alleviating bankrupt bed-sheets

Everyone has an opinion   Beware those
who have an opinion about everything

A cocaine psychosis pranks his sanity
When hallucinations arrive they always bring lunch

Waves of desire break on morality's reef

141

Fasting for -oscopies   I eat my hunger
taste the emptiness inside it   scoured & sour

Need now to begin & end each day stretching
Rubber bands hanging on doorknobs rot

A porch light all night glows   a minor star   Yes
the universe is right here   skin of the skin you move in

Hike leaf drizzle to realize transience
At this moment so much becoming something else

I fall weightlessly into your eyes' black holes

142

High in her eyes' sky-blue without art
or pleasure buzzards gyre keen for my heart

Dawn's light diffuses like watercolors laid wet
on wet pale pigments feathering sky's tooth

A Triscuit knock-off box tricks my eye
ethically-challenged capitalist *Trump*-l'oeil

Gisele Bundchen I want to be your yoga mat
I've no money but can help you spend yours

I sip my wine & taste the stars

143

Sensing light & heat beyond my smoot   a wasp
cold-stunned & clutching a screen poses for mortality

When the letter arrives its author has died
The hand's weight in the signature haunts the page

I thought I'd lost you   but with electric arabesques
on my eyelid screens you return   smiling like a newlywed

Fall reveals a hornet's hive hanging like an enemy's
branch-skewered head   vision of the world unseen

The sun intones in Latin lukewarm waves of prayer

144

When she mentions *forever*   cut up your credit cards
hide your checkbook & change all your passwords

Fall sun   friend not foe   engenders daydreams
the diluted warmth of its hand laving my face

What happened to youth's solitudes' candescent
relief   retreat from people & their *want   want   want*

Into the slowly curing concrete of your flesh
passing years like children scribe their names

You smell blackouts rising in whiskey's fumes

145

Despite December's argent haze & drizzle dazzling
me dizzy   dampness rots affection & breeds mold

My house is cold   refrigeration for a soul
shrinking from its vision of the final hole

The house settles   Crepitations clamber like rats
over joists & beams   creaks like burglars jimmy locks

A chatbot tells me there is not only not
someone for everyone but no one for most

No staying home for the *holidaze* alone

146

In deference to profits   Big Bizz today exploits consumers
whose frugality won't heat their winter homes

What good my 2-percent cash-back credit-card
when businesses now add 3-percent for me to use it

Capitalism evolves from supply & demand to zip-code
pricing   Adam Smith's *invisible hand* giving us the finger

Bizness will soon monetize the atmosphere
& we will all before long pay dearly to breathe

You hoard & roll coins again to buy your bread & wine

147

America's ceaseless renovations make it seem
the lives we lead are made of steam

Sometimes I feel I've never been me   want
to make *wrong* beautiful in a world of red lights

Not much more autocratic than progress erasing
my past & replacing it with melancholy & suspicion

Movies set during my kiddom estrange me from it
a past as foreign & defunct as Phisohex & Edsels

Memory   Dan   paints a version of not-quite-having-been

148

Six-thirty pitch-black winter solstice morning
& sounds ring like metal on an anvil beat

Yesterday   today   tomorrow then
yesterday   today   tomorrow then

Snagged in an oak Mylar balloon shreds tickle
the eye with scintillations of perpetual tinsel

Sirens whoop & whine tonight for Santa touring
neighborhoods atop a fire truck   sled on steroids

Open that wine   I'm not waiting to die

149

An ivy leaf glints as wind in sunlight turns it
nature's signal-lamp flashing code few will decipher

A student   once a lovely girl   you meet years later
& understand she was always a beautiful woman

Post-holidays & riding the opiates of solitude you wrestle
transcendence & lose   feel banality in you begin to nestle

Stars shiver in the freeze & a dog's bark breaks
like crystal or ice on a lake before you fall through

Vineyard roots under snow begin now to plump grapes

150

Many of us displaced refugees from Time   my child
-hood   houses razed   schools disappeared   gentrified

I awake from a dream of ants battling
feel them crawl along my every nerve

Postmodern sophists wield political power   & protean
selves   no slaves to truth   shift to express new fictions

Coalitions rankle the rank & file but on the beach
a breeze makes the sea-foam quiver

Rain's truth   Dan   slides down your throat like wine

After: What and Why the Ghazal, nearly a gazelle

Their are many definitions of this ancient Arabic form: "A ghazal may be understood as a poetic expression of both pain of loss or separation and the beauty of love in spite of that pain." So states a writer for Wikipedia. A traditional ghazal has a strict form: "independent but linked". There is a form to the poems, a limit but not a restraint. It is more similar in its improvised play to jazz than to a ballad, more loose than a sonnet.

Americans are insular, provincial, myopic. Even in their poetry they proclaim "America First" and "Freedom" which is little more than permission to suppress others; for poetry "free verse" denies history and proclaims the dominate and insular ego or individual expressiion reflecting the present time making of history merely a "pastime". These poems acknowlege and honor the tradition writers have learned from, learned and developed from the past to the present. And these poems are a present, a distant present of an old form made new.

But what of the near-Ghazal? Traditions remain, but altered, making the far near. The ghazal continues from the 7th century in slightly near-forms into the present. And it is a present, that many fine poets have given us, a gift from poets who reject the poetry advertising slogan Make it New, and look to honor

through near-imitation a near-flattery of past poetics and with that make the poem relevant and real. These poets, only a few: Federico Gacia Lorca, W. S. Merwin, Jim Harrison, Maxine Kumin, John Hollander, Dan Giancola.

An explanation of the oral roots of the ghazal, the oral roots of poetry:

The word "ghazal" originates from the Arabic word (gazal).

The root syllables Gh-Z-L have three possible meaning in Arabic.

To sweet-talk, to flirt, to display amorous gestures.

A young graceful doe (this is the root of the English word "gazelle").

To spin (thread or yarn).

This last meaning is similar to the origin of English "weave": "to lace together", "combine into a whole", "to go by twisting and turning", "a pattern of weaving". "to weave, warp, devise, produce".

What better description of poetry?. It's what a poem could be, should be, what these poems of Dan Giancola are: these near-ghazals. Near and dear.

They are derived from the past, but they are a present to us. Open them up to yourselves.

—Joe Napora, publisher of BullHead Books.

BullHead Books
2023

Made in the USA
Middletown, DE
13 April 2023

28737965R00091